Pasta

IN ITALIAN!

Marieluise Christl-Licosa

The varieties of Italian pasta are almost inexhaustible. Rigatoni, tortellini, spaghetti, lasagne and cannelloni are just a few among many to choose from. Then there is the huge variety of Italian sauces to go with them. Combined with pasta, they come top of the list of our favourite dishes. With plain tomato sauce, exquisite pesto sauce or a lavish lamb ragú, they are perfect to serve on any occasion.

Colour photography by
Odette Teubner and Kerstin Mosny

AURA

CONTENTS

Pasta in history

There must be something extraordinary about pasta because intelligent people are still fighting about which country first produced this simple type of food. It is certain that people in East and South-east Asia have been eating dishes made from noodle – or pasta – dough for thousands of years. However, there are very different opinions about where European pasta originated. There is a widespread view that Marco Polo brought it back to Genoa from one of his journeys to China, but there are also records of Jewish merchants having been there before him and it is thought that they took pasta to Eastern Europe. An American encyclopedia informs the astonished reader that Europe got to know pasta products through the Mongol invasions. Marco Polo wrote his travel accounts in 1298, but the history of Italian pasta is demonstrably older than this. An Etruscan grave has been found that contained an image of utensils that are necessary for making pasta. A Roman gourmet wrote in the first century that his table companions enjoyed eating "lasagna", baked pasta strips that were sweetly seasoned.

During the three centuries that followed, the cooking technique changed: the dough was left to dry a little, then it was cut into pasta and boiled in chicken stock. According to the chronicler, pasta had to be eaten fresh because it easily spoiled. The Arabs seem to have developed the idea of rolling the dough on sticks and leaving it to dry in the air. This was the birth of macaroni. However, the Sicilians claim that they gave this method to the Arabs. Although Sicilians have long been nicknamed "*mangimaccaroni*" (macaroni-eaters), whereas the Neapolitans were called "*mangiafoglie*" (vegetable-eaters), Naples can claim the ultimate credit for the triumphant progress of pasta. When pasta began to be made by machine, Naples developed a vigorous industry, which quickly made pasta the Italian national dish and for a long time supplied both the Old and New World with spaghetti.

The most famous kinds of pasta

The Italian word *pasta*, with which we are all familiar, comes from *pasta asciutta* and simply means dough or paste products. *Pasta asciutta* means dry pasta, as opposed to *pasta in brodo*, pasta cooked in broth.

Home-made tomato purée: Apulian housewives often make it themselves. The tomato purée is repeatedly smoothed out and thickened by the warmth of the sun before being stored.

Who can count and name all the different kinds of pasta? In order to help you, we have provided a key to the numbers in the illustration under the heading "The most famous kinds of pasta".

Both have always been served as a starter in Italy, usually at lunch time, and are now frequently served as a filling main course in many other countries throughout the world.

A distinction is made between long and short pasta. A favourite among the former is thin, round pasta, especially spaghetti (9). Spaghetti with the smallest diameter is called *capellini* or *vermicellini* (21). The next thickness up is called *vermicelli* (19) or *spaghettini*. Extra long spaghetti is almost always produced in Italy only

for export. Long pasta can be rectangular as well as round, without being as flat as ribbon noodles. The broader kind is called *tagliarini* (23); those that are somewhat narrower are called *linguine* or *trenette* (5). *Tagliatelle* (17) or *pappardelle* are ribbon-like, flat pasta. There is also hollow or tubular pasta of varying diameter. The scale begins with the relatively thin *buccatini* (8), continues through *macaroni* (7), *mezzanelli* up to *zitoni* (6). Short pasta can be thick or thin, cut straight or slanting, smooth or ridged. The

commonest kinds are *penne*, literally "quills" (11), and *ditali*, little thimbles (12), of various sizes, *rigatoni*, large, usually ridged, pasta tubes (10), and *conchiglie, smooth or ridged* shells (13). There are also *farfalle*, bows (14), *ruote*, wheels (15) and *gnocchi*, little dumplings (24). In the illustration above you can also see: *cannelloni* (1), *lasagne* (2), *pipe rigate* (3), *fusilli* (4), *tortellini* (16), *ravioli* (20) and *paglia e fieno* (22). They all appear in the recipes that follow. There are also many kinds of small pasta, which can be added to soups, such as *stellette*, little stars, *anellini, pepe bucato* and alphabet and numerals, which are favourites with children.

Nature creates a still life with fish in a small fishing port. Do not forget that there are many delicious pasta dishes made with fish and seafood.

Cooking Rule 1: "al dente"

I met a very old Neapolitan woman, who had been preparing pasta almost daily during the lifetimes of three generations. I asked her what to look out for if I wanted to cook pasta following all the rules. She did not think a foreigner would understand much about cooking, so she taught me from the beginning. If you follow the advice of this experienced cook exactly, you will succeed with the recipes in this book and nothing at all will go wrong, even at your very first attempt.

The most important rule of all is to boil pasta correctly. In a large saucepan bring 4 litres/7 pints water with 40 g/1 1/2 oz salt and about 5–10 ml/1–2 teaspoons olive oil to the boil. As soon as the water is bubbling, add 400 g/14 oz dried pasta all at once, stir well with a fork and cover until the water nearly boils over. Remove the lid and lower the heat a little, but the cooking process must not be interrupted for a single second. From time to time, stir the pasta well, so that it does not stick to the base of the saucepan. Test a piece at intervals to ensure the pasta does not overcook. It should be strained immediately it is just "al dente". *Al dente* means " to the tooth" – that is, tender, but still firm to the bite. It should never be too soft. My adviser was particularly strict

Wholemeal pasta

People today are increasingly turning to food that, as far as possible, remains in its natural state, so they reject refined flour. However, they do not have to give up eating pasta because a wide variety of types of wholemeal pasta is available in supermarkets and health food shops. A wholefood, rather than just wholemeal, pasta is also quite easy to make at home.

Grind 400 g/14 oz wheat to flour (or have it ground in the health food shop). Sift out enough bran to leave a remainder of 300 g/11 oz flour (otherwise the pasta will be too solid and heavy).

Mix the flour with 15 ml/1 tablespoon low-fat soya flour and form it into a small heap on a work surface. Make a well in the centre and add 2 lightly beaten eggs, 75 ml/5 tablespoons lukewarm water and 10 ml/2 teaspoons herb salt. Gradually mix the dry ingredients together with the liquid until fully incorporated, then knead the dough well until it is smooth, elastic and no longer sticks to the work surface. Shape it into a ball and brush with oil. Cover with an inverted bowl and set aside for 1 hour. Then continue following the basic recipe for pasta (pages 8–9).

about this point. She demanded that the strainer should be standing ready beside the saucepan, so that the pasta can be drained immediately it has reached exactly the right degree of tenderness and then mixed with the sauce.

Pasta cooking times

It is not possible to be absolutely precise about the exact time for cooking because pasta varies and some types take longer than others. The following times are guidelines, but keep checking, especially when cooking very thin fresh pasta. Calculate the cooking time from the moment the water returns to the boil after the pasta has been added.

Filled pasta:
Fresh 8–10 minutes
Dried 15–20 minutes

Unfilled pasta:
Fresh 2–3 minutes
Dried 8–12 minutes

The pasta machine

When you have once eaten home-made pasta, in future you and your family will not want to eat it any other way. In this case, you should buy a pasta machine. Electric machines have recently come on to the market, imported from Italy. They work beautifully, but are a nuisance to clean and, in any case, buying a fully automatic machine is only worthwhile

for a large Neapolitan family that eats pasta every day. For years I have made my own pasta with a simple hand-turned machine, which was recommended to me by Italian friends. Meanwhile, we have made various trips to the shop to buy accessories to make spaghetti and for filling and cutting out ravioli, However, the most important function of this apparatus is to make it easier to knead the dough. Cutting up the pasta also then becomes much easier.

If you do not have a fully automatic machine, knead the dough by hand until it is no longer sticky. Roll it out to about 2 cm/³/₄ inch thick and lightly dust each side with flour. Set the rollers at the widest setting. First fold the dough over three ways, press it flat, and feed it lengthways through the machine several times, until it is flat and shiny. Keep reducing the setting of the rollers. Feed the dough through until it is has acquired the right thickness. Be careful that long strips of dough do not fold over each other. Then cut the sheets of

dough in half across and feed them through the selected cutting roller. Continue according to the recipe for home-made pasta (see pages 8–9).

How to be an expert at eating pasta

Small boys in Italy laugh when they see foreigners eating spaghetti and getting it into a tangle. On the other hand, a foreigner may feel pure envy at seeing the breathtaking speed with which an Italian puts way a gigantic mountain of "pasta asciutta". The art of eating spaghetti properly has to be learned.

Spaghetti and other long pasta, such as tagliatelle, must be wound around something. There is no greater sin than cutting it into smaller pieces with your knife. Italians eat their spaghetti with just a fork. They pick up two or three strands with the prongs, pull them up from the tangle on the plate and then wind them round the fork at the edge of the plate. It does not matter if, in your haste, you leave a strand or two hanging from your mouth and then suck them up between your lips until they disappear.

So I hope you enjoy learning this art and have fun trying out all the recipes in this book.

Buon appetito!

Impression of Sicily – after the harvest oregano is bundled and taken to market.

Basic pasta dough

Easy

This basic recipe is international. I got it from my South Tyrolean grandmother, a very clever and capable woman. Generally speaking, she served her family and servants only home-made pasta. "It just tastes better," she said and, as always, had an appropriate saying on the tip of her tongue. "A spaghetti board and an excuse are both useful household tools!" Translated, this means a pasta board and a good excuse are necessary for peace in the home. She also told me, "It is easy to make your own pasta. You just have to take time to do it and the air in the kitchen should not be too dry. Otherwise the dough breaks. That is why before I set to work I brew myself a big pot of coffee and then everything works like a dream!"

Serves 4
400 g/14 oz plain flour
4 eggs
salt
extra flour or water, if necessary

Approximately per portion:
2,000 kJ/480 kcal
25 g protein, 14 g fat
68 g carbohydrate

● Approximate preparation
  time: 2¹⁄₂ hours of which
  1 hour is standing time

1. Sift the flour on to a work surface so that it forms a small heap. With your hand, make a large well in the centre.

2. Add the eggs and a pinch of salt. Using a fork and working from the inside outwards, mix the eggs with the flour until the mixture becomes crumbly.

3. Quickly knead the mixture into a dough. Keep kneading with the palms of your hands for a further 10–15 minutes, until the dough is smooth and shiny.

4. If the dough does not bind, add a little water. If it sticks or is too soft, then work in a little more flour. When you cut the dough, there must be no holes on the cut surface. Then it is ready.

5. Loosely wrap the dough in a clean tea towel. Cover with an inverted bowl and leave to stand for about 15 minutes.

6. Lightly sprinkle the work surface with flour. Divide the dough into 3–4 portions and roll it out with a rolling pin, always working from the centre to the edge, until it is about the thickness of the back of a knife blade. Keep the dough that you have not yet rolled out wrapped in a tea towel.

7. Leave the sheets of dough to dry for 5–10 minutes, then lightly sprinkle with flour, roll it out and use a knife to cut it into the desired widths. Alternatively, feed the dough through a pasta machine, selecting the right roller for the width you want (see also page 7).

8. Carefully pick up the pasta, using both hands, shake it and let it fall loosely on to a floured tea towel. Leave it to dry on the tea towel for at least 1 hour. Note: fresh pasta has a much shorter cooking time than dried pasta (see page 7).

Variations:

Lasagne and cannelloni

For lasagne, cut the dough into 8 x 12 cm/3 x 5 inch rectangles. For cannelloni, cut it into 12 x 12 cm/5 x 5 inch squares. Leave the rectangles and the squares to dry for about 1 hour, then cook them in salted water. Stack the rectangles on top of each other with a layer of filling between each. Cover the squares with the filling and roll up. Bake both specialities in the oven with *sugo*, a sauce.

Pasta verde (green pasta)

Briefly blanch 400 g/14 oz spinach in boiling water. Rinse it in cold water and squeeze out as much moisture as possible. Either rub it through a strainer with the back of a wooden spoon or process in a food processor to form a purée. Work the spinach into a dough with 400 g/14 oz plain flour, 2 eggs and a pinch of salt. If necessary, knead in more flour. When you roll it out, keep sprinkling the work surface with flour.

Pasta rossa (red pasta)

Prepare the dough with 400 g/14 oz plain flour, 3 eggs, 65–75 g/2^1/$_2$–3 oz tomato purée (according to the intensity of the colour you want) and a pinch of salt.

Pasta gialla (yellow-orange pasta)

Prepare the pasta dough using the basic recipe. Knead in 2 g/^{1}/$_{16}$ oz ground saffron.

Home-made ravioli and tortellini

Easy

Serves 4
For the filling:
1 onion
1 clove garlic
45 ml/3 tablespoons olive oil
350 g/12 oz minced beef or lamb
2.5 ml/^{1}/$_2$ teaspoon finely chopped
    fresh rosemary or a pinch of
    dried rosemary
5–10 ml/1–2 teaspoons finely
    chopped fresh thyme or
    2.5 ml/^{1}/$_2$ teaspoon dried thyme
120 ml/4 fl oz beef stock
For the dough:
400 g/14 oz plain flour
4 eggs
salt and freshly ground white pepper

Approximately per portion:
3,200 kJ/760 kcal
41 g protein, 35 g fat
69 g carbohydrate

● Approximate preparation
  time for the ravioli: 2^1/$_2$ hours
  of which 1 hour is
  standing time

● Approximate preparation
  time for the tortellini: 3 hours
  of which 1 hour is
  standing time

1. Finely chop the onion and garlic. Heat the oil and sauté them until translucent. Add the meat and cook, stirring frequently, until browned all over. Stir in the herbs and season to taste. Add the stock, cover and simmer for 20 minutes. Remove the lid and cook over a strong heat until all the liquid has evaporated. Remove the pan from the heat and set aside to cool.

2. Make the pasta dough as described on pages 8–9. Cover with an inverted bowl and leave it to stand for about 15 minutes.

3. For ravioli, divide the dough into two portions and roll them out into sheets about the thickness of the back of a knife blade.

4. Place small heaps of the filling about 4 cm/1^1/$_2$ inches apart on one sheet of dough. Lightly brush the other dough sheet with a little water and, with this side downwards, place it carefully on top of the first sheet.

5. Press the spaces between the filling firmly with your finger. Then cut out the ravioli into small squares with a pasta wheel or a round pastry cutter.

6. For the tortellini, roll out all the pasta dough to about 1–2 cm/ $^1/_2$–$^3/_4$ inch thick and cut out circles or squares about 5–6 cm/ 2–2$^1/_2$ inches in diameter or length. Put a small heap of the filling on the middle of each shape.

7. Brush half the sides with water. Shape the circles into half moons and the squares into triangles with the corners pointing up. Press the edges firmly together. Then bend them into rings around the tip of your index finger and press the ends firmly together.

8. Boil the ravioli or tortellini for about 10 minutes in salted water. You can prepare the ravioli the day before and keep it in the refrigerator, but then it will take twice as long to cook.

Filling variations:

With chicken and bacon

Cut 115 g/4 oz each skinned chicken breast fillet and pork fillet into small cubes and fry them well in 15 g/$^1/_2$ oz butter. Then mince or process in a food processor, together with 115 g/4 oz bacon and 50 g/2 oz Mortadella. Add 115 g/4 oz freshly grated Parmesan cheese and 1 egg. Season well with salt, freshly ground black pepper and freshly grated nutmeg.

With spinach and ricotta cheese

Wash and partially dry 350 g/ 12 oz spinach. Cook in a covered saucepan over a low heat until the leaves wilt. Drain thoroughly, squeezing out as much liquid as possible, and leave to cool, then finely chop. Finely chop 200 g/7 oz ricotta cheese. Mix well with the spinach, 50 g/2 oz freshly grated Parmesan cheese and 1 egg. Season with freshly ground black pepper and freshly grated nutmeg.

Minestrone alla milanese

Thick Milan vegetable soup

Rather time-consuming

Serves 4
150 g/5 oz dried white beans
1 onion
1 small celery stick
25 g/1 oz butter
15 ml/1 tablespoon olive oil
15 ml/1 tablespoon tomato purée
about 1.5 litres/2¹/2 pints stock
   (see Tip)
1 leek
2 medium carrots
2 small courgettes
2 medium potatoes
¹/4 small Savoy cabbage
1 clove garlic
1 bunch parsley
2 fresh sage leaves
75 g/3 oz rindless, streaky bacon
115–150 g/4–5 oz dried ziti or
   other small pasta shapes
150 g/5 oz frozen peas
45 ml/3 tablespoons freshly grated
   Parmesan cheese
salt and freshly ground black pepper

Approximately per portion:
2,400 kJ/570 kcal
24 g protein, 27 g fat
61 g carbohydrate

● Soaking time: about 12 hours
● Approximate preparation
time: 2¹/2 hours of which
2 hours are cooking time

1. Put the beans in a bowl, cover with cold water and set aside to soak for at least 12 hours.

2. Finely chop the onion and thinly slice the celery.

3. Heat the butter and oil in a large saucepan. Add the onion and celery and sauté over a medium heat for about 5 minutes, until translucent.

4. Mix the tomato purée with 750 ml/1¹/4 pints of the stock and add to the pan. Drain the beans and add to the pan. Bring the soup to the boil.

5. Cut the leek in half lengthways, then into slices. Dice the carrots, courgettes and potatoes. Remove and discard the cabbage stalk and cut the leaves into thin strips. Add the carrots, courgettes, potatoes and cabbage to the pan. Cover and simmer over a low heat for 1¹/2 hours.

6. Finely chop the garlic, parsley, sage leaves and bacon and mix together well to form a paste. Add the remaining stock to the pan and stir in the bacon paste. Simmer over a low heat for a further 15 minutes.

6. Increase the heat, add the pasta and peas and cook until the pasta is tender, but still firm to the bite. Stir in the grated Parmesan cheese, season to taste with salt and pepper and serve immediately.

Tip

To make stock, put soup bones, meat trimmings, thyme, parsley, celery, onion, carrot and 1–2 bay leaves into a large saucepan. Cover with cold water and bring to the boil. Remove the scum that rises to the surface with a slotted spoon. Simmer for 2 hours over a low heat. Strain the stock through a fine strainer or a strainer lined with clean muslin, discarding the vegetables, bones, meat trimmings and flavourings. Cool and store in the refrigerator or use at once.

This soup has it all – eight different kinds of vegetables are assembled in Minestrone alla milanese.

Minestra di pasta e piselli

Pea soup with pasta

Good value

Serves 4
1 small onion
1 small carrot
1/2 bunch parsley
1 small stick celery
50 g/2 oz rindless streaky bacon
30 ml/2 tablespoons olive oil
15 ml/1 tablespoon tomato purée
150 ml/1/4 pint water
about 1.5 litres/2 1/2 pints vegetable
    stock
200 g/7 oz frozen peas
115–150 g/4–5 oz dried quadrucci
    or other small pasta shapes
50 g/2 oz freshly grated
    Parmesan cheese
salt

Approximately per portion:
1,500 kJ/360 kcal
16 g protein, 18 g fat
34 g carbohydrate

● Approximate preparation
  time: 1 hour

---

1. Finely chop the onion, carrot, parsley and celery stick. Finely dice the bacon.

2. Heat the oil in a large saucepan. Add all the vegetables and the bacon and sauté, stirring constantly, over a medium heat for about 5 minutes.

3. Mix together the tomato purée and water and stir into the saucepan. Cover and simmer for

about 10 minutes. Pour in the stock and bring to the boil. Stir the peas and pasta into the soup and cook until the pasta is tender, but still firm to the bite. Season to taste with salt. Transfer to warm individual soup bowls and serve immediately, sprinkled with Parmesan cheese.

Minestra di lenticchie

Lentil soup with pasta

Easy

Serves 4
250 g/9 oz brown lentils
1.5 litres/2 1/2 pints water
1 large onion
1 stick celery
2 cloves garlic
1 bunch parsley
75 g/3 oz rindless streaky bacon
4 beefsteak tomatoes
60 ml/4 tablespoons olive oil
225 g/8 oz dried ditali or other
    small pasta shapes
45 ml/3 tablespoons freshly grated
    pecorino cheese
salt and freshly ground black pepper

Approximately per portion:
2,700 kJ/640 kcal
30 g protein, 26 g fat
72 g carbohydrate

● Soaking time: about 12 hours
● Approximate preparation
  time: 1 1/2 hours

---

1. Rinse the lentils, transfer to a bowl and add the water. Set aside to soak overnight.

2. Cut the onion in half horizontally. Cut one onion half into rings. Cut the celery in half.

3. Transfer the lentils, together with their soaking water, to a saucepan. Add the onion rings and half the celery. Bring to the boil, lower the heat, cover and simmer for about 1 1/2 hours.

4. Finely chop the garlic, parsley, bacon, remaining onion and remaining celery.

5. Heat the oil in a large saucepan. Add the garlic, parsley, bacon, onion and celery and sauté over a medium heat for about 5 minutes. Add the tomatoes, cover and simmer over a medium heat for about 15 minutes.

6. Add the lentils to the pan, together with their cooking water. If the soup is too thick, add a little more water. Season to taste with salt and pepper.

7. When the lentils are just cooked, remove and discard half the celery. Add the pasta to the soup and boil until it is tender, but still firm to the bite. Stir in the grated pecorino cheese, transfer to warm serving bowls and serve immediately.

Above: Minestra di pasta e piselli
Below: Minestra di lenticchie

Minestra con zucchini

Courgette soup

Easy

Serves 4
1 onion
500 g/1 1/4 lb small firm courgettes
1/2 bunch parsley
1/2 bunch basil
500 g/1 1/4 lb beefsteak tomatoes
90 ml/6 tablespoons olive oil
1.5 litres/2 1/2 pints stock
* (see Tip, page 12)*
200 g/7 oz dried ditali or other
* small pasta shapes*
salt and freshly ground white pepper
115 g/4 oz freshly grated Parmesan
* cheese, to serve*

Approximately per portion:
1,900 kJ/450 kcal
21 g protein, 22 g fat
43 g carbohydrate

● Approximate preparation
  time: 1 hour

---

1. Finely chop the onion. Cut the courgettes lengthways into quarters, then dice finely. Finely chop the parsley and basil leaves together.

2. Briefly blanch the tomatoes in boiling water. Peel, seed and coarsely chop the flesh.

3. Heat the olive oil in a large saucepan. Add the onion and sauté over a medium heat, stirring occasionally, until soft and translucent. Add the courgettes and sauté, stirring occasionally, for a further 5 minutes. Stir in the mixed fresh herbs and tomatoes. Cover the saucepan and simmer over a medium heat for about 30 minutes.

4. Bring the stock to the boil in another saucepan. Pour the boiling stock into the pan with the courgettes. Season to taste with salt and pepper. Add the ditali or other pasta and boil until it is tender, but still firm to the bite. Transfer to warm soup bowls and serve immediately with the Parmesan cheese.

Minestra con pomodori

Tomato soup with pasta

Good value

Serves 4
3 cloves garlic
2 sticks celery
1 bunch parsley
12 large basil leaves
400 g/14 oz can tomatoes
75–90 ml/5–6 tablespoons olive oil
pinch of ground peperoncino or
* cayenne pepper*
about 1.5 litres/2 1/2 pints stock
* (see Tip, page 12)*
150–200 g/5–7 oz dried ziti or
* other small pasta shapes*
salt
90 g/3 1/2 oz freshly grated
* Parmesan cheese, to serve*

Approximately per portion:
1,700 kJ/400 kcal
17 g protein, 20 g fat
39 g carbohydrate

● Approximate preparation
  time: 1 1/2 hours

---

1. Finely chop the garlic. Thinly slice the celery. Finely chop the parsley and coarsely chop the basil. Rub the tomatoes, together with their can juice through a strainer with the back of a wooden spoon.

2. Heat the oil in a large saucepan. Add the garlic, celery and herbs and sauté over a medium heat for about 5 minutes. Add the tomatoes to the pan and season well with the peperoncino or cayenne pepper. Cover and simmer over a low heat for about 15 minutes.

3. Bring the stock to the boil in a saucepan, then pour it into the tomato mixture. Season to taste with salt. Cover and simmer over a low heat for about 45 minutes.

4. Increase the heat, add the pasta and boil, stirring frequently, until it is tender, but still firm to the bite. Transfer to warm soup bowls and serve immediately with grated Parmesan cheese.

Above: Minestra con pomodori
Below: Minestra con zucchini

PASTA – PLAIN BUT EXQUISITE

Ditali con mozzarella

Pasta with tomatoes and mozzarella

Exquisite • Vegetarian

Serves 4
500 g/1 1/4 lb plum tomatoes
200 g/7 oz mozzarella cheese
1 bunch fresh basil
*30 ml/2 tablespoons extra virgin
    olive oil*
*ground peperoncino or
    cayenne pepper*
2 cloves garlic
*400 g/14 oz dried ditali or other
    pasta shapes*
*45 ml/3 tablespoons freshly grated
    Parmesan cheese*
25 g/1 oz butter
salt

Approximately per portion:
2,800 kJ/670 kcal
29 g protein, 28 g fat
71 g carbohydrate

● Approximate preparation
    time: 45 minutes

1. Briefly blanch the tomatoes in boiling water, then peel, seed and finely dice the flesh. Cut the mozzarella cheese into very small cubes and set aside. Finely chop the basil leaves.

2. Heat the oil in a large flameproof casserole. Add the garlic and fry over a medium heat until it is brown, then take it out. Add the tomatoes to the casserole and season to taste with salt and peperoncino or cayenne pepper.

Cover and simmer over a low heat for about 15 minutes.

3. Meanwhile, cook the pasta in salted boiling water until it is tender, but still firm to the bite. Then drain it and add to the tomatoes, together with the diced mozzarella. Stir until the cheese has melted. Mix in the grated Parmesan cheese, butter and basil and serve immediately straight from the casserole.

Spaghetti agli odori

Spaghetti with herbs and tomatoes

*Rather time-consuming •
Vegetarian*

Serves 4
600 g/1 lb 5 oz plum tomatoes
1 stick celery
1/2 onion
2 cloves garlic
1 bunch basil
1 bunch parsley
*5 ml/1 teaspoon fresh
    oregano leaves*
*75 ml/5 tablespoons extra virgin
    olive oil*
400 g/14 oz dried spaghetti
salt and freshly ground black pepper

Approximately per portion:
2,000 kJ/480 kcal
16 g protein, 13 g fat
74 g carbohydrate

● Approximate preparation
    time: 30 minutes
● Marinating time: about
    4 hours

1. Briefly blanch the tomatoes in boiling water. Peel, seed and finely dice the flesh.

2. Finely chop the celery, onion and garlic. Finely chop the basil, parsley and oregano leaves.

3. Mix together the tomatoes, celery, onion, garlic, basil, parsley, oregano and olive oil in a large bowl. Season well with salt and pepper. Cover and set aside to marinate for 4 hours.

4. Cook the pasta in salted boiling water until it is tender, but still firm to the bite. Drain and add to the bowl of tomatoes and herbs. Mix thoroughly and serve immediately.

*Above: Ditali con mozzarella
Below: Spaghetti agli odori*

Trenette al pesto genovese

Pasta with pesto

Elegant • Vegetarian

Serves 4
4 bunches basil
4 cloves garlic
30 ml/2 tablespoons pine nuts
about 120 ml/4 fl oz olive oil
75 g/3 oz freshly grated
   pecorino cheese
400 g/14 oz dried trenette,
   fettucine or spaghetti
salt and freshly ground
   white pepper

Approximately per portion:
3,600 kJ/860 kcal
25 g protein, 51 g fat
77 g carbohydrate

● Approximate preparation
   time: 1 hour

---

1. Roughly chop or tear the basil leaves. Crush or finely chop the garlic cloves.

2. Pound the basil leaves in a mortar with a little salt. Season to taste with pepper and add the garlic and pine nuts. Keep pounding with the pestle and gradually mix in the olive oil and the grated cheese, a spoonful at a time, until the mixture becomes smooth and creamy.

3. Alternatively, put the basil leaves, salt, pepper, garlic and pine nuts in a food processor and process until smooth. With the motor still running, gradually add the oil and grated cheese and process until the mixture is smooth and creamy.

4. Cook the pasta in salted boiling water until it is tender, but still firm to the bite. Drain, reserving 250 ml/8 fl oz of the cooking water, and transfer to a warm serving dish.

5. Stir the reserved cooking liquid into the pesto to dilute it slightly. Add the pesto to the pasta and toss well to coat, using two forks. Serve at once.

Spaghetti con aglio, olio e peperoncino

Spaghetti with garlic, oil and hot peppers

For guests • Vegetarian

Serves 4
400 g/14 oz dried spaghetti
5 cloves garlic
1 bunch parsley
90 ml/6 tablespoons olive oil
about 1 cm/1/2 inch dried
   peperoncino or 2 dried chillies
salt
60 ml/4 tablespoons freshly grated
   pecorino or Parmesan cheese,
   to serve

Approximately per portion:
2,200 kJ/520 kcal
20 g protein, 19 g fat
68 g carbohydrate

● Approximate preparation
   time: 30 minutes

---

1. Cook the spaghetti in salted boiling water until it is tender, but still firm to the bite.

2. Crush the garlic with a fork or the blade of a knife. Finely chop the parsley.

3. Heat the oil in a small frying pan, add the garlic and peperoncino or chillies. Fry over a medium heat until the garlic is golden brown, then remove both the garlic and peperoncino or chillies from the pan.

4. Drain the pasta, reserving 30–45 ml/2–3 tablespoons of the cooking water, and transfer to a warm serving dish.

5. Pour the hot garlic-flavoured oil over the pasta. If necessary, add the reserved cooking water. Sprinkle the pasta with parsley, mix well and serve at once with the grated cheese.

Above: Trenette al pesto genovese
Below: Spaghetti con aglio, olio e peperoncino

Penne al Gorgonzola

Pasta with Gorgonzola

Exquisite • Vegetarian

Serves 4
400 g/14 oz dried penne or
*   bucatini broken into pieces*
200 g/7 oz Gorgonzola cheese
25 g/1 oz butter
4–6 fresh sage leaves
250 ml/8 fl oz double cream
salt and freshly ground
*   white pepper*

Approximately per portion:
3,300 kJ/790 kcal
25 g protein, 45 g fat
69 g carbohydrate

● Approximate preparation
   time: 30 minutes

---

1. Cook the pasta in salted boiling water until it is tender, but still firm to the bite.

2. Meanwhile, cut the Gorgonzola cheese into small cubes.

3. Melt the butter in a heavy-based flameproof casserole over a low heat. Add the sage leaves, cook for a few seconds, then remove from the casserole. Add the cheese and stir over a low heat until it has melted. Gradually stir in two thirds of the cream. Season the cheese sauce to taste with salt and pepper and heat over a low heat until thickened.

4. Drain the pasta, add it to the casserole and toss to mix

well. If the dish becomes too dry, add the remaining cream. Serve immediately, garnished with the sage leaves.

Variation
For extra flavour, stir in 30 ml/ 2 tablespoons dry vermouth with the double cream in step 3.

Vermicelli al sugo di basilico

Thin pasta in basil sauce

Elegant • Vegetarian

Serves 4
3 bunches basil
400 g/14 oz dried vermicelli
*   or linguine*
115 g/4 oz butter
250 ml/8 fl oz double cream
40 g/1 1/2 oz freshly grated
*   pecorino cheese*
salt and freshly ground
*   white pepper*

Approximately per portion:
3,300 kJ/790 kcal
20 g protein, 46 g fat
72 g carbohydrate

● Approximate preparation
   time: 30 minutes

---

1. Finely chop the basil leaves or tear into very small pieces.

2. Cook the pasta in salted boiling water until it is tender, but still firm to the bite.

3. Meanwhile, melt the butter in a small saucepan over a medium

heat. Warm the cream in another small saucepan over a low heat.

4. Drain the pasta and transfer to a flameproof casserole or serving dish Add the melted butter, cream, basil and cheese and season to taste with salt and pepper. Cover and leave to stand on the still warm (not hot) hob for about 5 minutes, then serve.

Variation
You can also prepare this dish with the same amount of flat leaf parsley and, in addition, season the cream with nutmeg. This dish would look particularly attractive if prepared with green pasta or a mixture of plain and green pasta.

Above: Penne al Gorgonzola
Below: Vermicelli al sugo di basilico

Spaghetti con zucchini

Spaghetti with courgettes

Serves 4
1 onion
500g/1¹/4 lb small firm courgettes
¹/2 bunch basil
350 g/12 oz beefsteak tomatoes
75–90 ml/5–6 tablespoons olive oil
pinch of cayenne pepper
400g/14 oz dried spaghetti
salt
75 g/3 oz freshly grated pecorino
  cheese, to serve

Approximately per portion:
2,400 kJ/570 kcal
24 g protein, 21 g fat
75 g carbohydrate

● Approximate preparation
  time: 1 hour

---

1. Finely chop the onion. Dice the courgettes. Chop the basil. Briefly blanch the tomatoes, then peel, seed and finely chop the flesh.

2. Heat the olive oil in a saucepan. Add the onion and sauté over a medium heat for about 5 minutes. Add the courgettes and sauté for 2–3 minutes, then stir in the tomatoes. Season to taste with salt and cayenne pepper and add the basil. Cook the vegetables over a low heat until tender.

3. Cook the pasta in salted boiling water until it is tender, but still firm to the bite. Drain, add to the sauce and toss to coat. Transfer to a warm serving dish and serve immediately, with the cheese.

Maccheroni con broccolo

Macaroni with broccoli

For guests

Serves 4
50 g/2 oz sultanas
1 kg/2¹/4 lb broccoli
1 onion
2 cloves garlic
6 anchovy fillets
500g/1¹/4 lb beefsteak tomatoes
120 ml/4 fl oz olive oil
50 g/2 oz pine nuts
400g/14 oz dried macaroni
¹/2 bunch basil
65 g/2¹/2 oz freshly grated
  pecorino cheese
salt

Approximately per portion:
3,300 kJ/790 kcal
36 g protein, 34 g fat
90 g carbohydrate

● Approximate preparation
  time: 1³/4 hours

---

1. Put the sultanas in a bowl, cover with lukewarm water and set aside to soak for about 15 minutes.

2. Peel the broccoli stalks and cut deep crosses into the bottom of each one. Cook the broccoli in salted boiling water until just tender. Drain and divide into small florets.

3. Thinly slice the onion and push out into rings. Crush the garlic. Finely chop the anchovy fillets. Briefly blanch the tomatoes. Peel, seed and finely chop the flesh.

4. Heat half the olive oil. Add the onion and sauté over a low heat for about 5 minutes, until soft and translucent. Add the tomatoes and season to taste with salt. Cover and simmer for about 30 minutes. Then add the broccoli, cover and cook for 5–10 minutes.

5. Heat the remaining olive oil. Add the garlic and sauté over a low heat for about 5 minutes. Add the anchovies and sauté for about 2–3 minutes. Drain and squeeze the sultanas, add them to the pan, together with the pine nuts, and cook for a further 5 minutes.

6. Break the macaroni into 4–5 cm/1¹/2–2 inch long pieces. Cook in salted boiling water until it is tender, but still firm to the bite. Finely chop the basil or tear into very small pieces. Drain the pasta. First mix it with the anchovy sauce, then with the broccoli and tomato mixture. Transfer to a warm serving dish, sprinkle with the basil and cheese, toss to mix thoroughly and serve immediately.

Above: Maccheroni con broccolo
Below: Spaghetti con zucchini

Bucatini al cavolfiori

Bucatini with cauliflower

Exquisite

Whatever the the time of year, cauliflower is always in season! With this dish you can extend your culinary repertoire.

Serves 4
1 small cauliflower, about 600 g/
1 lb 5 oz
1 onion
2 cloves garlic
5 anchovy fillets
60 ml/4 tablespoons olive oil
pinch of saffron
pinch of ground peperoncino or
cayenne pepper
400g/14 oz dried bucatini or other
long, hollow pasta
salt
75 g/3 oz freshly grated pecorino
cheese, to serve

Approximately per portion:
2,400 kJ/570 kcal
30 g protein, 19 g fat
74 g carbohydrate

● Approximate preparation
time: 1 hour

1. Peel the cauliflower stalk and cut a 2 cm/³/₄ inch deep cross in the base. Cook in salted boiling water for about 15 minutes, until just tender. Finely chop the onion and garlic. Finely chop the anchovy fillets or crush them with a fork.

2. Heat the oil in a flameproof casserole. Add the onion and garlic and sauté over a low heat, stirring constantly, until soft and translucent. Add the anchovies and sauté, stirring with a fork, for 2–3 minutes, until the mixture becomes creamy.

3. Drain the cauliflower, reserving the cooking liquid. Divide the cauliflower into florets and add to the anchovy mixture. Dissolve the saffron in a little of the reserved cooking water, season with the peperoncino or cayenne pepper and add to the cauliflower. Cover and simmer over a low heat, stirring once, for about 5 minutes.

4. Cook the pasta in the remaining reserved cooking water, adding extra salted boiling water if necessary, until it is tender, but still firm to the bite. Drain, add to the casserole and toss to mix well. Turn off the heat, but do not remove the casserole. Cover and leave to stand on the hob for about 5 minutes. Serve with the grated cheese.

Spaghetti alla ciociara

Spaghetti with peppers

Easy • Vegetarian

This simple dish comes from Rome, where they have always preferred to serve pecorino, rather than Parmesan cheese, with pasta. You must definitely sprinkle this delicious spaghetti with this cheese, as it gives the dish its particular flavour.

Serves 4
1 onion
2 large yellow peppers
200 g/7 oz black olives
400g/14 oz can tomatoes
120 ml/4 fl oz olive oil
400g/14 oz dried spaghetti
75 g/3 oz freshly grated
  pecorino cheese
salt and freshly ground black pepper

Approximately per portion:
3,300 kJ/790 kcal
24 g protein, 43 g fat
78 g carbohydrate

● Approximate preparation
  time: 1 1/4 hour

1. Finely chop the onion. Core and seed the peppers and cut the flesh into 1 cm/¹/₂ inch wide strips. Stone and coarsely chop the olives. Drain the tomatoes and coarsely chop them.

2. Heat the oil in a saucepan. Add the onions and sauté over a medium heat, stirring constantly, for about 5 minutes, until they are soft and translucent. Add the tomatoes, peppers and olives and season to taste with salt and pepper. Cover and simmer over a low heat for 30–40 minutes.

3. Meanwhile, cook the pasta in salted boiling water until it is tender, but still firm to the bite. Drain the pasta and transfer to a warm serving bowl.

4. Add the sauce to the spaghetti and toss thoroughly. Cover and leave to stand for 3–4 minutes. Sprinkle with the pecorino and serve immediately.

Fusilli agli spinaci

Pasta spirals with spinach

Vegetarian

Serves 4
1 bunch parsley
1 bunch basil
about 750 g/1³/₄ lb young spinach
400g/14 oz dried fusilli
65 g/2¹/₂ oz butter
30 ml/2 tablespoons olive oil
pinch of freshly grated nutmeg
250 ml/8 fl oz double cream
75 g/3 oz freshly grated
   Parmesan cheese
salt

Approximately per portion:
3,400 kJ/810 kcal
27 g protein, 45 g fat
72 g carbohydrate

● Approximate preparation
   time: 1 hour

---

1. Finely chop the parsley and basil leaves.

2. Put the spinach into a flameproof casserole with no added water other than that clinging to the leaves after washing. Cook over a low heat until the leaves wilt. Strain thoroughly and set aside to cool, then press out as much liquid as possible and finely chop the leaves.

3. Cook the fusilli in salted boiling water until it is tender, but still firm to the bite.

4. Heat the butter and oil in a heavy-based saucepan. Add the herbs and sauté over a low heat for 2–3 minutes, then add the spinach. Season to taste with salt and grated nutmeg, mix well, cover and cook over a low heat for about 5 minutes.

5. Add the cream and heat through without boiling. Remove the casserole from the heat.

6. Drain the pasta and transfer to a warm serving dish. Add the spinach mixture and grated Parmesan cheese and toss well, using two large forks. Cover the bowl and leave to stand for 3–4 minutes before serving.

Penne al sugo di asparagi

Pasta with asparagus sauce

For guests • Vegetarian

Serves 4
1 stick celery
1 small carrot
1 small onion
400g/14 oz can tomatoes
750 g/1³/₄ lb green asparagus
75 g/3 oz butter
400g/14 oz dried penne
salt and freshly ground
   white pepper
50 g/2 oz freshly grated Parmesan
   cheese, to serve

Approximately per portion:
2,400 kJ/570 kcal
23 g protein, 22 g fat
75 g carbohydrate

● Approximate preparation
   time: 1 hour

---

1. Finely chop the celery, carrot and onion. Drain the tomatoes, reserving the juice, and coarsely chop them.

2. Cut off the white ends of the asparagus. If necessary, peel the lower end of the stalks of the green asparagus. Cut the asparagus stems into 4 cm/1¹/₂ inch long chunks, leaving the asparagus tips about 4–5 cm/1¹/₂–2 inches long.

3. Melt the butter in a large saucepan. Add the celery, carrot and onion and sauté over a medium heat, stirring constantly, for about 10 minutes. Then add the asparagus and sauté for 5 minutes.

4. Stir in the tomatoes and season to taste with salt and pepper. Cover and simmer over a low heat for 15–20 minutes. If necessary, add a little of the reserved tomato can juice.

5. Meanwhile, cook the pasta in salted boiling water until it is tender, but still firm to the bite. Drain and transfer to a warm serving dish. Add the asparagus, cover and leave to stand for 2–3 minutes before serving with the Parmesan cheese.

Above: Fusilli agli spinaci
Below: Penne al sugo di asparagi

Maccheroni al pomodoro

Macaroni with tomato sauce

Easy • Vegetarian

Serves 4
1 onion
$^1/_2$ bunch basil
2 x 400 g/14 oz cans tomatoes
105 ml/7 tablespoons olive oil
pinch of ground peperoncino or
*   cayenne pepper*
pinch of sugar
1 bay leaf
400g/14 oz dried macaroni, broken
*   into short lengths*
salt
75 g/3 oz freshly grated Parmesan
*   cheese, to serve*

Approximately per portion:
2,500 kJ/600 kcal
23 g protein, 23 g fat
75 g carbohydrate

● Approximate preparation
  time: 1 hour

---

1. Finely dice the onion. Coarsely chop the basil or tear the leaves into small pieces. Put the tomatoes, together with their can juice, into a bowl and mash them with a fork.

2. Heat 75 ml/5 tablespoons of the olive oil in a flameproof casserole. Add the onion and sauté for about 5 minutes, until soft and translucent. Add the tomatoes, together with their juice. Season to taste with salt, peperoncino or cayenne pepper and sugar and add the bay leaf and basil. Cook,

uncovered, over a low heat until the sauce has thickened.

3. Meanwhile, cook the pasta in salted boiling water until it is tender, but still firm to the bite. Drain thoroughly.

4. Remove and discard the bay leaf. Mix the remaining olive oil into the sauce. Add the pasta and, if necessary, heat through. Serve immediately with the grated Parmesan cheese,

Tagliatelle ai funghi

Ribbon pasta with mushrooms

Exclusive • Vegetarian

Serves 4
2 cloves garlic
400g/14 oz can tomatoes
75 ml/5 tablespoons extra virgin
*   olive oil*
2.5 ml/$^1/_2$ teaspoon dried oregano
400g/14 oz mushrooms, preferably
*   wild mushrooms, such as ceps,*
*   or a mixture of cultivated and*
*   wild mushrooms*
400g/14 oz dried tagliatelle or
*   pasta spirals*
salt and freshly ground white pepper
115 g/4 oz freshly grated Parmesan
*   cheese, to serve*

Approximately per portion:
2,400 kJ/570 kcal
26 g protein, 20 g fat
71 g carbohydrate

● Approximate preparation
  time: 45 minutes

---

1. Finely chop the garlic. Drain the tomatoes and mash with a fork.

2. Heat 30 ml/2 tablespoons of the olive oil in a flameproof casserole. Add the garlic and sauté over a medium heat for about 5 minutes. Add the tomatoes and season to taste with salt and pepper and stir in the oregano. Cook, uncovered, over a low heat for about 20 minutes, until the sauce has thickened.

3. Slice the mushrooms. Heat the remaining oil in a large frying pan. Add the mushrooms and cook over a high heat until all the liquid has been driven off.

4. Stir the mushrooms into the tomato sauce and season to taste with salt and pepper. Cover and simmer over a low heat for 10 minutes.

5. Meanwhile, cook the pasta in salted boiling water until it is tender, but still firm to the bite. Drain and transfer to a warm serving dish. Add the mushroom sauce and toss to mix well. Serve immediately with the grated Parmesan cheese.

Above: Tagliatelle ai funghi
Below: Maccheroni al pomodoro

Spaghetti alle vongole

Spaghetti with clams

Rather time-consuming

A favourite with many holiday-makers in Italy. Fresh clams are available in season, but you can substitute canned – good enough reason to enjoy this famous dish at home from time to time.

Serves 4
1 kg/2¹/₄ lb clams
90 ml/6 tablespoons olive oil
1 small onion
3 cloves garlic
about 12 large basil leaves
350 g/11 oz beefsteak tomatoes
pinch of ground peperoncino or
*   cayenne pepper*
400 g/14 oz dried spaghetti
salt

Approximately per portion:
2,300 kJ/550 kcal
22 g protein, 20 g fat
72 g carbohydrate

● Approximate preparation
   time: 1³/₄ hour

1. Scrub the clams thoroughly under cold running water. Discard any that do not shut immediately when sharply tapped with a knife or that have broken shells. Drain the clams well. Put them into a saucepan with 15 ml/1 tablespoon of the oil and cover.

2. Cook over a high heat, shaking the pan from time to time, for about 10 minutes, until the clams have opened. Drain, reserving the cooking liquid, and discard any clams that have not opened.

3. Finely chop the onion and crush the garlic. Finely chop the basil or tear the leaves into small pieces.

4. Briefly blanch the tomatoes in boiling water. Peel, seed and finely chop the flesh.

5. Heat the remaining oil. Add the onion and sauté, stirring constantly, for about 5 minutes. Add the garlic and basil and sauté for about 2 minutes, but do not allow the garlic to become brown. Add the tomatoes, cover and simmer over a medium heat for about 30 minutes.

6. Strain the reserved cooking liquid through a strainer lined with muslin to remove any sand. Then add it to the tomato sauce. Season with peperoncino or cayenne pepper and salt if required.

7. Cook the spaghetti in salted boiling water until it is tender, but still firm to the bite. Meanwhile, remove the clams from their shells and add them to the tomato sauce. Heat through for about 2–3 minutes.

8. Drain the pasta well and transfer to a warm serving dish. Add the clam sauce, toss to mix and serve immediately.

Variation

Spaghetti alle vongole in bianco

Crush 6 cloves garlic with a fork or a broad-bladed knife. Heat 90 ml/ 6 tablespoons olive oil in a large frying pan. Add the garlic and a piece of peperoncino and fry until the garlic is nearly black. Remove the garlic and peperoncino. Prepare the clams as above and add them to the pan. Cover and cook until the shells have opened. Meanwhile, cook the spaghetti until it is tender, but still firm to the bite. Drain, reserving 60 ml/ 4 tablespoons of the cooking water, and transfer to individual warm plates. Add the reserved cooking liquid to the clams. Top the spaghetti with the clams in their shells, together with the cooking liquid. Sprinkle over finely chopped parsley and serve. A bowl for empty shells and finger bowls with paper napkins would be advisable.

Spaghetti con le seppie

Spaghetti with squid sauce

Exclusive

Squid are not only excellent grilled or fried. They can lend an exquisite touch to a plain pasta dish.

Serves 4
500 g/1¼ lb prepared fresh or
*   frozen squid*
400 g/14 oz can tomatoes
1 onion
2 cloves garlic
1 stick celery
1 carrot
1 bunch parsley
1 sprig rosemary or a pinch of
*   dried rosemary*
75 ml/5 tablespoons olive oil
40 g/1½ oz butter
60–90 ml/4–6 tablespoons dry
*   white wine or vegetable stock*
400 g/14 oz dried spaghetti
salt and freshly ground black pepper

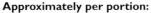

Approximately per portion:
3,000 kJ/710 kcal
35 g protein, 27 g fat
78 g carbohydrate

● Approximate preparation
  time: 2 hours

1. Thaw the squid, if frozen. Cut the tentacles into pieces and the bodies into 5 mm/¼ inch wide strips or rings.

2. Drain the tomatoes and rub them through a strainer with the back of a wooden spoon. Alternatively, process in a food processor to a smooth purée.

3. Finely chop the onion and crush the garlic. Thinly slice the celery. Coarsely grate the carrot. Finely chop the parsley and the fresh rosemary, if using.

4. Heat 60 ml/4 tablespoons of the olive oil and the butter in a flameproof casserole. Add the onion, garlic, celery and carrot and sauté over a medium heat for about 5 minutes.

5. Add the chopped squid tentacles, cover and sauté over a medium heat for about 20 minutes, until they are nearly tender, adding a little white wine from time to time.

6. Add the parsley and rosemary and cook, uncovered, for about 5 minutes. Stir in the squid strips or rings and cook, stirring constantly, for 4–5 minutes. Add the tomatoes and season to taste with salt and pepper. Cover and

simmer over a low heat for 30 minutes–1 hour, according to size, until tender.

7. Meanwhile, cook the spaghetti in salted boiling water with the remaining oil until it is tender, but still firm to the bite. Drain and transfer to a warm serving dish.

8. Add the squid to the dish of spaghetti, toss with two large forks to mix thoroughly and serve immediately.

In northern regions of Italy good squid recipes have a rarity value. With Spaghetti con le seppie you can embellish your recipe repertoire.

Spaghetti con i gamberetti

Spaghetti with prawns

For guests

Serves 4
350 g/12 oz peeled prawns, fresh
*   or frozen*
3 cloves garlic
5 sprigs basil
1/2 bunch parsley
300 g/11 oz beefsteak tomatoes
115 g/4 oz butter
400 g/14 oz dried spaghetti
*   or bucatini*
15 ml/1 tablespoon olive oil
salt and freshly ground
*   white pepper*

Approximately per portion:
2,600 kJ/620 kcal
27 g protein, 25 g fat
72 g carbohydrate

● Approximate preparation
   time: 45 minutes

---

1. Thaw the prawns, if frozen. Finely chop the garlic. Finely chop the basil and parsley separately. Briefly blanch the tomatoes. Peel, seed and finely chop the flesh.

2. Coarsely chop the prawns. Heat the butter in a saucepan. Add the garlic and sauté over a low heat, stirring constantly for about 5 minutes, until golden. Stir in the prawns. Add the tomatoes and the basil and season to taste with salt and pepper. Cover and simmer over a low heat for about 15 minutes.

3. Cook the spaghetti or bucatini in salted boiling water with the oil until it is tender, but still firm to the bite. Drain the pasta and transfer to four individual warm serving dishes. Top with the parsley and the prawn sauce and serve immediately.

Spaghetti al sugo de pesce

Spaghetti with Sicilian fish sauce

Exquisite

Serves 4
450 g/1 lb firm-fleshed fish fillets,
*   such as trout or snapper*
juice of 1 lemon
2 cloves garlic
50 g/2 oz stoned green olives
3 anchovy fillets
15 ml/1 tablespoon capers
1 bunch parsley
400 g/14 oz can tomatoes
75 ml/5 tablespoons extra virgin
*   olive oil*
120 ml/4 fl oz dry white wine
pinch of ground peperoncino or
*   cayenne pepper*
400 g/14 oz dried spaghetti
15 ml/1 tablespoon olive oil
salt

Approximately per portion:
2,700 kJ/640 kcal
39 g protein, 20 g fat
74 g carbohydrate

● Approximate preparation
   time: 1 hour

---

1. Sprinkle the fish with the lemon juice. Crush the garlic. Coarsely chop the olives. Finely chop the anchovies, capers and parsley. Drain the tomatoes, reserving the can juice, and rub them through a strainer with the back of a wooden spoon.

2. Heat the oil. Add the garlic, olives, anchovies and capers and sauté over a low heat for about 5 minutes. Add the wine and cook, stirring constantly, over a medium heat until reduced. Add the tomatoes and peperoncino or cayenne pepper and season to taste with salt. Cover and simmer for about 15 minutes. If the mixture is becoming too dry, add a little of the reserved tomato juice. Fold in the parsley. Lightly salt the fish fillets and add them to the sauce. Cover and cook over a low heat, turning the fish once, for 10 minutes

3. Cook the spaghetti in salted boiling water with the oil until it is tender, but still firm to the bite. Drain and transfer to a warm serving dish.

4. Break up the fish with two forks and mix it into the sauce. Add the sauce to the spaghetti, toss to mix well and serve immediately.

Above: Spaghetti con i gamberetti
Below: Spaghetti al sugo de pesce

Spaghetti al tonno e pomodori

Spaghetti with tuna and tomatoes

Good value

Italians love eating fish. On the coast it is easy to get seafood of all kinds. However, people living inland had to learn the art of preserving fish, so they created countless recipes for "sugo al tonno", tuna fish sauce.

Serves 4
2 cloves garlic
4 anchovy fillets
200 g/7 oz can tuna fish in oil
400 g/14 oz can tomatoes
45 ml/3 tablespoons extra virgin olive oil
pinch ground peperoncino or cayenne pepper
30–45 ml/2–3 tablespoons vegetable stock, if required
1 bunch parsley
400 g/14 oz dried spaghetti
salt

Approximately per portion:
2,400 kJ/570 kcal
29 g protein, 19 g fat
71 g carbohydrate

● Approximate preparation time: 50 minutes

1. Finely chop the garlic with the anchovy fillets. Drain the tuna and mash it with a fork. Coarsely chop the tomatoes.

2. Heat the olive oil. Add the garlic and anchovies and sauté over a low heat for about 5 minutes. Add the tuna and season with the peperoncino or cayenne pepper and salt to taste. Cook for a further 5 minutes. Add the tomatoes and cook, uncovered, over a medium heat for about 20 minutes, until thickened.

3. If the sauce becomes too thick, add the vegetable stock. Finely chop the parsley and stir it into the sauce shortly before the end of the cooking time. Season the sauce again, if necessary.

4. Cook the spaghetti in salted boiling water until it is tender, but still firm to the bite. Drain and add it to the sauce. Cover and leave to stand on the hob with the heat turned off for a further 2–3 minutes. You can also serve the pasta and sauce separately.

Spaghetti alla puttanesca

Spaghetti in spicy tomato and anchovy sauce

Exquisite

This speciality originated on the island of Ischia. It is simply exquisite and extraordinarily delicious! That is why a long time ago it spread from its island home all over the Italian mainland. If you do not yet know it, you really must try it!

Serves 4
3 cloves garlic
8–10 anchovy fillets
150 g/5 oz black olives
15–30 ml/1–2 tablespoons capers
500 g/1 1/4 lb beefsteak tomatoes
90–120 ml/6–8 tablespoons olive oil
pinch of ground peperoncino or
*   cayenne pepper*
400 g/14 oz dried spaghetti
salt

Approximately per portion:
3,000 kJ/710 kcal
26 g protein, 38 g fat
75 g carbohydrate

● Approximate preparation
    time: 1 hour

1. Thinly slice the garlic. Finely chop the anchovy fillets. Stone the olives and chop coarsely. Finely chop the capers.

2. Briefly blanch the tomatoes in boiling water. Peel, seed and coarsely chop the flesh.

3. Heat the oil in a saucepan. Add the garlic and sauté over a low heat. Add the anchovies and crush them with a fork. Add the olives, capers and tomatoes. Season with salt and add the peperoncino or cayenne pepper. Cover and simmer over a low heat for 30 minutes.

4. Meanwhile, cook the pasta in salted boiling water until it is tender, but still firm to the bite. Drain and transfer to a warm serving dish. Add the sauce, toss well to mix and serve immediately.

Conchiglie al pesce

Pasta shells with fish sauce

Exquisite

Serves 4
1 carrot
2 onions
3 sprigs parsley
$^1/2$ bay leaf
4 peppercorns
1 litre/1$^3/4$ pints water
5 ml/1 teaspoon lemon juice
500 g/1$^1/4$ lb whole cod
3 cloves garlic
5 anchovy fillets
120 ml/4 fl oz olive oil
22.5 ml/4$^1/2$ teaspoons tomato
   purée
15 ml/1 tablespoon olive oil
400 g/14 oz dried conchiglie
45 ml/3 tablespoons dry Marsala
salt and freshly ground white pepper

Approximately per portion:
2,800 kJ/670 kcal
41 g protein, 22 g fat
75 g carbohydrate

● Approximate preparation
   time: 1$^1/2$ hours

1. Slice the carrot. Cut 1 onion into eight equal-size pieces.

2. Put the carrot, onion pieces, parsley, bay leaf and peppercorns into a medium-size saucepan and add the water. Bring to the boil, cover and cook for 20 minutes. Add the lemon juice and season with salt.

3. Add the fish to the pan, cover and simmer over a low heat for about 20 minutes, until you can remove the fins. Lift the fish out of the pan and set aside to cool. Strain the cooking liquid and reserve 120 ml/4 fl oz.

4. Finely chop the remaining onion. Thinly slice the garlic. Finely chop the anchovies.

5. When cold enough to handle, remove and discard the skin, fins and bones from the fish and finely chop the flesh.

6. Heat 75 ml/5 tablespoons of the olive oil in a flameproof casserole. Add the chopped onion and sauté over a medium heat, stirring constantly, for about 5 minutes, until soft and translucent. Add the fish and sauté for a further 5 minutes.

7. Mix together the tomato purée and the reserved fish stock to a smooth paste and add to the casserole. Cover and simmer over a very low heat for about 10 minutes.

8. Meanwhile, heat 30 ml/ 2 tablespoons of the remaining olive oil in a small frying pan. Add the garlic and sauté over a low heat until it is golden. Add the anchovy fillets and stir with a fork until the mixture becomes creamy.

9. Cook the pasta in salted boiling water with the remaining oil until it is tender, but still firm to the bite. Drain well.

10. Add the anchovy sauce to the fish sauce. Stir in the Marsala and then season to taste with salt and pepper.

11. Mix the pasta into the casserole with the fish sauce. Cover and leave to stand on the hob with the heat switched off for 2–3 minutes. Although it is not really authentic, this dish looks attractive if you serve the sauce and pasta separately.

Fish does not only go with chips. It can be delicious with pasta too. The proof – Conchiglie al pesce.

Spaghetti alla carbonara

Spaghetti with bacon and eggs

Easy

Serves 4
150 g/5 oz pancetta or rindless
    streaky bacon
3 cloves garlic 30 ml/2 tablespoons
    olive oil
400 g/14 oz dried spaghetti
3 eggs
50 g/2 oz freshly grated
    pecorino cheese
50 g/2 oz freshly grated
    Parmesan cheese
salt and freshly ground
    white pepper

Approximately per portion:
3,700 kJ/880 kcal
36 g protein, 53 g fat
70 g carbohydrate

● Approximate preparation
  time: 40 minutes

---

1. Finely dice the pancetta or bacon. Heat the oil in a large, heavy-based frying pan. Add the garlic and sauté over a medium heat until it is well browned. Then remove it from the pan and discard. Add the pancetta or bacon and fry until it is crisp. Set aside and keep warm.

2. Meanwhile, cook the spaghetti in salted boiling water until it is tender, but still firm to the bite.

3. Lightly beat together the eggs, pecorino cheese and Parmesan

cheese and season to taste with salt and pepper.

4. Drain the spaghetti. Quickly mix it with the pancetta or bacon in the frying pan. Then remove the pan from the hob. Add the egg mixture and quickly mix together with two large forks until all the pasta is coated. Serve immediately. (It is important to have all the cooked ingredients piping hot and to work quickly so that the eggs cook immediately on contact.)

Bucatini alla calabrese

Bucatini with bacon and tomatoes

Easy

Serves 4
3 cloves garlic
1 carrot
1 stick celery
about 12 large basil leaves
150 g/5 oz rindless streaky bacon
400 g/14 oz beefsteak tomatoes
60 ml/4 tablespoons olive oil
pinch of ground peperoncino
or cayenne pepper
400 g/14 oz dried bucatini
    or spaghetti
salt
50 g/2 oz freshly grated Parmesan
    cheese and 50 g/2 oz freshly
    grated pecorino cheese, to serve

Approximately per portion:
3,100 kJ/740 kcal
31 g protein, 35 g fat
74 g carbohydrate

● Approximate preparation
  time: 1 hour

---

1. Crush the garlic. Finely chop the carrot and celery. Coarsely chop the basil leaves or tear into small pieces. Dice the bacon.

2. Heat the oil in a flameproof casserole. Add the garlic, carrot and celery and sauté over a medium heat, stirring constantly, for 8–10 minutes.

3. Meanwhile, briefly blanch the tomatoes. Peel, seed and coarsely chop the flesh.

4. Add the bacon to the casserole and fry over a low heat for about 5 minutes. Stir in the tomatoes. Season to taste with salt and add the peperoncino or cayenne pepper and the basil. Cover and simmer over a low heat for 15–20 minutes.

5. Meanwhile, cook the pasta in salted boiling water until it is tender, but still firm to the bite. Drain, add to the casserole and toss well with two large forks to mix. Transfer to a warm serving dish and serve immediately with the grated cheese.

Above: Spaghetti alla carbonara
Below: Bucatini alla calabrese

Rigatoni con ragù di maiale

Rigatoni with pork

Serves 4
400 g/14 oz can tomatoes
1 bunch basil
2 onions
400 g/14 oz boneless
 pork shoulder
45 ml/3 tablespoons olive oil
pinch of ground peperoncino or
 cayenne pepper
400 g/14 oz dried rigatoni
 or macaroni
salt
65 g/2 1/2 oz freshly grated pecorino
 cheese, to serve

Approximately per portion:
3,400 kJ/810 kcal
38 g protein, 40 g fat
74 g carbohydrate

● Approximate preparation
 time: 1 3/4 hours

---

1. Rub the tomatoes through a strainer with the back of a wooden spoon. Coarsely chop the basil or tear the leaves into small pieces. Finely chop the onion. Dice the pork into 1 cm/1/2 inch cubes.

2. Heat 30 ml/2 tablespoons of the olive oil. Add the onion and sauté over a medium heat for about 5 minutes. Add the pork, a little at a time and cook over a high heat, stirring constantly, until browned all over. Add the tomatoes and the basil. Season to taste with salt and stir in the peperoncino or cayenne pepper. Cover and cook over a low heat

for about 1 hour. If the mixture is becoming too dry, add a little hot water.

3. Cook the rigatoni in salted boiling water with the remaining oil, until it is tender, but still firm to the bite. Drain and serve with the sauce. Hand the grated pecorino cheese separately.

Pasta alla bolognese

Pasta with meat sauce

Rather time-consuming

Serves 4
1 small onion
1 small carrot
1 stick celery
50 g/2 oz rindless streaky bacon
400 g/14 oz can tomatoes
60 ml/4 tablespoons olive oil
20 g/3/4 oz butter
200 g/7 oz minced beef
115 g/4 oz minced pork
50 ml/2 fl oz dry red wine
75 ml/5 tablespoons beef stock
1 clove
1 bay leaf
freshly grated nutmeg
400 g/14 oz dried spaghetti
75 g/3 oz freshly grated
 Parmesan cheese
salt and freshly ground black
 pepper

Approximately per portion:
3,500 kJ/830 kcal
39 g protein, 43 g fat
73 g carbohydrate

● Approximate preparation
 time: 1 3/4 hours

---

1. Finely chop the onion, carrot and celery. Finely dice the bacon. Drain the tomatoes, reserving the can juice, and mash them roughly with a fork.

2. Heat the olive oil and the butter. Add the onion and sauté for about 5 minutes. Add the carrot, celery and bacon and cook for a further 5 minutes.

3. Add the minced beef and minced pork and fry over a high heat, stirring constantly, for about 5 minutes. Add the wine and cook until reduced. Pour in the beef stock and bring to the boil. Stir in the tomatoes.

4. Season to taste with salt and pepper and stir in the clove, bay leaf and nutmeg. Stir thoroughly and simmer over a very low heat for 1 hour. If the sauce is becoming too dry, add a little of the reserved tomato can juice.

5. Cook the pasta in salted boiling water until it is tender, but still firm to the bite. Transfer to a warm serving dish, top with the sauce and grated Parmesan cheese and serve immediately.

Above: Bolognese sauce
Below: Rigatoni con ragù di maiale

Lasagne alla molisana

Baked pasta with Italian sausage sauce

For guests

Serves 4
1 onion
3 cloves garlic
400 g/14 oz can tomatoes
15 ml/1 tablespoon tomato
  purée
about 115 g/4 oz butter, softened,
  plus extra for greasing
pinch of ground peperoncino or
  cayenne pepper
4–5 eggs
300 g/11 oz mozzarella cheese
115 g/4 oz pancetta or smoked
  streaky bacon
300 g/11 oz Italian pork sausage,
  such as cotechino, cervellata
  or luganeghe
120 ml/4 fl oz dry white wine or
  beef stock
15 ml/1 tablespoon olive oil
350 g/12 oz lasagne
50 g/2 oz freshly grated
  pecorino cheese
50 g/2 oz freshly grated
  Parmesan cheese
salt

Approximately per portion:
6,100 kJ/1,500 kcal
66 g protein, 99 g fat
68 g carbohydrate

● Approximate preparation
  time: 2 hours

---

1. Finely chop the onion and the garlic. Rub the tomatoes, together with their juice, through a strainer with the back of a wooden spoon and then mix them with the tomato purée.

2. Heat 25 g/1 oz of the butter. Add the onion and garlic and sauté over a low heat, stirring constantly, for about 8 minutes. Add the tomatoes and season to taste with salt. Stir in the peperoncino or cayenne pepper, bring to the boil over a low heat and simmer.

3. .Meanwhile, prick the eggs at the round ends and boil them for about 10 minutes, until hard. Rinse in cold water, shell and finely dice. Finely dice the mozzarella and the pancetta or streaky bacon. Skin the sausage and mash the sausage meat well with a fork.

4. Melt 10 g/^{1}/$_4$ oz butter in a heavy-based frying pan over a low heat. Add the pancetta or bacon and the sausage meat and fry, stirring constantly, over a medium heat for 5 minutes. Pour in the wine or stock and cook, stirring frequently, until reduced. Stir in the tomato mixture, cover and simmer over a low heat for about 15 minutes.

5. If you are using lasagne sheets that need pre-cooking, prepare them, a few at a time, according to the packet instructions.

6. Preheat the oven to 200°C/400°F/Gas 6. Thoroughly grease a rectangular ovenproof dish with butter.

7. Put a layer of lasagne on the base of the dish, then cover with a layer of the tomato and sausage sauce. Top with some diced mozzarella and egg and sprinkle with Parmesan cheese and pecorino cheese. Repeat this layering process until all the ingredients have been used up, except for a few spoons of sauce and some cheese.

8. Spread the remaining sauce evenly over the top, sprinkle with the remaining cheese and dot with the remaining butter.

9. Bake for 30–35 minutes, until cooked through. Serve the lasagne immediately.

The housewives in the Molisa region (near the Abruzzi) are specialists in heartily spiced dishes, as is shown in Lasagne alla molisana.

Paglia e fieno

Coloured ribbon pasta with bacon and cream

Easy

Serves 4
150 g/5 oz lean boiled bacon
*   or ham*
400 g/14 oz dried mixed green and
*   plain tagliatelle*
75 g/3 oz butter
200 ml/7 fl oz double cream
115 g/4 oz freshly grated
*   Parmesan cheese*
freshly grated nutmeg
salt and freshly ground white pepper

Approximately per portion:
3,400 kJ/810 kcal
31 g protein, 47 g fat
69 g carbohydrate

● Approximate preparation
   time: 20 minutes

---

1. Dice the bacon or ham into very small cubes. Cook the pasta in salted boiling water until it is tender, but still firm to the bite. Drain well.

2. Melt the butter in a large flameproof casserole. Add the cream and stir in the grated Parmesan cheese. Season to taste with grated nutmeg, salt and pepper.

3. Add the bacon or ham and pasta to the sauce and mix together well. Cover and simmer over a very low heat for 1–2 minutes until heated through. Serve immediately.

Pappardelle all'aretina

Pappardelle with duck

For guests

Serves 4
1 small oven-ready duck
1 onion
1 clove garlic
1 carrot
1 stick celery
115 g/4 oz rindless streaky bacon
1 bunch parsley
4 sage leaves
1 sprig rosemary
1 sprig thyme
45 ml/3 tablespoons olive oil
1 bay leaf
105 ml/7 tablespoons dry
*   white wine*
15 ml/1 tablespoon tomato purée
105 ml/7 tablespoons chicken stock
400 g/14 oz dried pappardelle
salt and freshly ground black pepper
65 g/2 1/2 oz freshly grated
*   Parmesan cheese, to serve*

Approximately per portion:
7,000 kJ/1,700 kcal
100 g protein, 110 g fat
72 g carbohydrate

● Approximate preparation
   time: 2 1/2 hours

---

1. Divide the duck into 8–10 pieces. Finely chop the onion, garlic, carrot, celery and bacon. Finely chop the parsley, sage, rosemary and thyme or pound them in a mortar with a pestle.

2. Heat the oil in a very large flameproof casserole (if necessary, use two casseroles). Add the onion, garlic, carrot, celery and bacon and sauté over a medium heat, stirring constantly, for about 5 minutes. Add the chopped herbs and the bay leaf. Arrange the duck pieces side by side in the casserole and fry over a medium heat, turning once or twice, for about 10 minutes, until they are golden brown all over.

3. Pour in the white wine and keep turning the duck in it until the wine has reduced by half.

4. Stir together the tomato purée and the stock to a smooth paste, then pour the mixture into the casserole. Season to taste with salt and pepper, stir thoroughly and simmer over a low heat for 1 1/4–1 1/2 hours.

5. Cook the pasta in salted boiling water until it is tender, but still firm to the bite. Drain well. Remove the duck from the casserole with a slotted spoon and keep warm. Add the pasta to the sauce and mix well. Return the duck pieces to the casserole and serve immediately with the grated Parmesan cheese.

Above: Duck sauce for Pappardelle all'aretina
Below: Paglia e fieno

Lasagne alla contessa

Lasagne with mixed meat and mozzarella

For guests

This recipe was given to me by a countess from Bologna with whom I made friends.

Serves 4
1 onion
1 large carrot
1 stick celery
50 g/2 oz rindless pancetta or
*   streaky bacon*
400 g/14 oz can tomatoes
350 g/12 oz lean mixed minced
*   meat or 175 g/6 oz each veal*
*   and pork escalope*
about 115 g/4 oz butter, plus extra
*   for greasing*
105 ml/7 tablespoons strong dry
*   red wine*
about 105 ml/7 fl oz veal or
*   beef stock*
about 600 ml/1 pint milk
50 g/2 oz plain flour
300 g/11 oz mozzarella cheese
15 ml/1 tablespoon olive oil
about 300 g/11 oz lasagne
75 g freshly grated
*   Parmesan cheese*
salt and freshly ground
*   white pepper*

Approximately per portion:
5,700 kJ/1,400 kcal
62 g protein, 80 g fat
80 g carbohydrate

● Approximate preparation
  time: $3^3/4$ hours of which
  about $2^3/4$ hours are cooking
  time

---

1. Finely chop the onion, carrot, celery and pancetta or bacon. Put the tomatoes, together with their can juice, into a food processor and process to a purée. Alternatively, rub them through a strainer with the back of a wooden spoon.

2. If using escalopes, finely dice the meat. Melt 50 g/2 oz of the butter and fry the pancetta or bacon. Add the vegetables and sauté until the onion is soft and translucent. Add the meat and fry, stirring frequently, until well browned. Pour in the red wine and cook over a medium heat, stirring constantly, until reduced. Pour in half the veal or beef stock and simmer over a low heat. Gradually add in the remaining stock and cook until reduced.

3. Stir in the tomatoes. Season to taste with salt and pepper and pour in enough milk just to cover (about 250 ml/8 fl oz). Simmer over a low heat for at least 2 hours. If necessary, add more stock.

4. For the Béchamel sauce, melt 50 g/2 oz of the remaining butter in a saucepan. Stir in the flour and cook briefly. Gradually stir in the remaining milk, beating the mixture vigorously with a whisk. Season to taste with salt and pepper. Do not allow the sauce to become too thick. If necessary, stir in a little more milk.

5. Dice the mozzarella into small cubes.

6. If using lasagne that needs pre-cooking, prepare it according to the packet instructions.

7. Pre-heat the oven to 180°C/350°F/Gas 4. Thoroughly grease a rectangular ovenproof dish with butter.

8. Arrange a layer of lasagne in the prepared dish. Spoon in a layer of meat sauce, cover with mozzarella and then top with Béchamel sauce. Sprinkle with Parmesan cheese and season with pepper. Repeat this process until all the ingredients have been used up, ending with a covering of Béchamel sauce. Sprinkle the remaining Parmesan on top. Dot the top with the remaining butter. Bake for 30–40 minutes, until cooked through. Serve immediately.

This dish is a lasagne with an aristocratic background – Lasagne alla contessa tastes superb.

Tagliatelle al cervo

Tagliatelle with venison

Exclusive

Serves 4
1 onion
2 cloves garlic
2 carrots
1 stick celery
75 g/3 oz rindless pancetta or
*   streaky bacon*
45–60 ml/3–4 tablespoons olive oil
750 g/1 lb 10 oz boneless leg or
*   shoulder of venison*
400 g/14 oz can tomatoes
pinch of freshly grated nutmeg
1 bay leaf
2 cloves
pinch of dried thyme
120 ml/4 fl oz hot beef stock
400 g/14 oz dried tagliatelle
15 g/1/2 oz butter
salt and freshly ground black pepper
45 ml/3 tablespoons freshly grated
*   Parmesan cheese, to serve*

Approximately per portion:
3,700 kJ/880 kcal
61 g protein, 37 g fat
75 g carbohydrate

● Approximate preparation
   time: 2 1/2–3 hours

---

1. Finely chop the onion, garlic, carrot and celery. Finely dice the pancetta or bacon.

2. Dice the venison into 2–3 cm/ 3/4–1 inch cubes. Heat the oil in a large saucepan. Add the meat, a little at a time, and fry over a high heat until browned all over.

Remove the venison from the pan. Add the onion, garlic, carrots, celery and pancetta or bacon and sauté, stirring occasionally for about 10 minutes.

3. Add the tomatoes, together with their can juice, and mash them with a fork. Season to taste with salt and pepper and stir in the nutmeg, bay leaf, cloves and thyme. Return the meat to the pan and add the hot beef stock. Cover and cook over a low heat for 1 1/2–2 hours.

4. Cook the pasta in salted boiling water until it is tender, but still firm to the bite. Drain thoroughly, toss with the butter and transfer to warm individual serving plates. Top the pasta with the venison sauce and serve immediately. Hand the Parmesan cheese separately.

Macheroni con ragù d'agnello

Macaroni with lamb sauce

For guests

Serves 4
750 g/1 lb 10 oz boneless shoulder
*   of lamb*
1 onion
2 sticks celery
2 x 400 g cans tomatoes
90 ml/6 tablespoons extra virgin
*   olive oil*
120 ml/4 fl oz dry white wine
pinch of ground peperoncino or
*   cayenne pepper*
2 bay leaves
400 g/14 oz dried macaroni
salt
50 g/2 oz freshly grated pecorino
*   cheese, to serve*

Approximately per portion:
5,100 kJ/1,200 kcal
49 g protein, 77 g fat
76 g carbohydrate

● Approximate preparation
   time: 2 hours

---

1. Dice the lamb into 1 cm/1/2 inch cubes. Finely chop the onion and celery. Drain the tomatoes, reserving the can juice, and coarsely chop.

2. Heat 75 ml/5 tablespoons of the oil. Add the lamb and fry over a high heat until browned all over. Add the onion and celery and cook for a further 5 minutes.

3. Add the wine and cook, stirring constantly, until reduced. Add the tomatoes. Add the peperoncino and bay leaves and season to taste with salt. Cover and cook over a low heat for 1 1/2 hours. If the mixture is becoming too dry, add some of the reserved tomato can juice.

4. Break the pasta into pieces 4–5 cm/1 1/2–2 inches long. Cook in salted boiling water with the remaining oil until it is tender, but still firm to the bite. Drain well. Serve immediately with the lamb sauce and hand the grated pecorino cheese separately.

Above: Tagliatelle al cervo
Below: Macheroni con ragù d'agnello

Cannelloni

Stuffed pasta rolls

For guests

Serves 4
2 small onions
2 cloves garlic
400 g/14 oz can tomatoes
1 bunch parsley
90 ml/6 tablespoons olive oil
250 g/9 oz spinach
115 g/4 oz rindless boiled bacon
350 g/12 oz minced beef
2 eggs
115 g/4 oz freshly grated
    Parmesan cheese
20 cannelloni tubes
50 g/2 oz butter, plus extra
    for greasing
25 g/1 oz plain flour
150–175 ml/5–6 fl oz milk
salt and freshly ground white pepper

Approximately per portion:
4,300 kJ/1,000 kcal
54 g protein, 63 g fat
65 g carbohydrate

● Approximate preparation
time: 2¹/₄ hours

1. Finely chop the onions. Crush the garlic. Put the tomatoes, together with their can juice in a bowl and mash with a fork. Finely chop the parsley.

2. Heat 45 ml/3 tablespoons of the oil in a flameproof casserole. Add half the onions, half the garlic and the parsley and sauté over a medium heat for about 5 minutes. Add the tomatoes. Season to taste with salt and pepper, cover and simmer over a low heat for 30 minutes.

3. Meanwhile, put the spinach in a saucepan with just the water clinging to the leaves after washing and cook until it wilts. Drain, squeeze out as much water as possible and finely chop the leaves. Finely dice the bacon.

4. Heat the remaining oil. Add the remaining onion and garlic and sauté over a medium heat for about 5 minutes. Increase the heat, add the beef and fry, stirring constantly, for 5 minutes. Transfer the mixture to a bowl, mix with the spinach and bacon and set aside to cool.

5. When the beef and spinach mixture is cool, stir in the eggs and half the grated Parmesan cheese and season to taste with salt and pepper.

6. If the cannelloni needs pre-cooking, prepare it according to the packet instructions.

7. To make the Béchamel sauce, melt half the butter. Stir in the flour and cook briefly. Gradually add the milk, stirring constantly,

with a whisk. Season to taste with salt and pepper.

8. Preheat the oven to 200°C/400°F/Gas 6. Thoroughly grease a rectangular ovenproof dish with butter.

9. Stuff the cannelloni with the meat and spinach mixture.

10. Spread half the tomato sauce over the base of the prepared dish. Arrange 10 cannelloni tubes side by side on top. Spoon half the Béchamel sauce over the pasta. Arrange the remaining cannelloni tubes in a second layer, cover with the remaining tomato sauce and top with the remaining Béchamel sauce. Sprinkle the remaining Parmesan cheese on top. Dot the remaining butter over the surface. Bake the cannelloni for about 20–30 minutes, until the cheese has melted and is lightly browned. Serve immediately.

This cannelloni has a rich filling of spinach, bacon, minced meat and eggs.

Crostata ai funghi

Baked pasta and mushrooms

Easy

Serves 4
300 g/11 oz mushrooms
115 g/4 oz fontina cheese
150 g/5 oz butter
50 g/2 oz plain flour
500 ml/17 fl oz milk
freshly grated nutmeg
350 g/12 oz dried tagliarini
2 egg yolks
45 ml/3 tablespoons freshly grated
*   Parmesan cheese*
salt and freshly ground white pepper

Approximately per portion:
4,200 kJ/1,000 kcal
38 g protein, 63 g fat
74 g carbohydrate

● Approximate preparation
  time: 1 hour

1. Slice the mushrooms. Cut the fontina cheese into thin slices.

2. Melt 50 g/2 oz of the butter. Add the flour and cook, stirring constantly, until it is golden. Gradually add the milk, beating vigorously with a whisk. Season to taste with salt, pepper and nutmeg. Bring the sauce to the boil, add the fontina cheese and cook until it has melted. Remove the pan from the heat. Preheat the oven to 220°C/400°F/Gas 6.

3. Melt 25 g/1 oz of the remaining butter; add the mushrooms and cook over a low heat for 10 minutes. Meanwhile, cook the pasta in salted boiling water until tender, but still firm to the bite. Drain, return to the pan and add 50 g/2 oz of the remaining butter, the egg yolks and one third of the cheese sauce. Fold in the mushrooms, with some of their cooking juices.

4. Grease an ovenproof dish with the remaining butter. Put the pasta into it. Pour on the remaining cheese sauce and smooth the top. Sprinkle with the Parmesan cheese. Bake for about 15 minutes, until it is golden brown.

Frittata con i gamberetti

Pasta omelette with prawns

Easy

This way of preparing spaghetti as an omelette goes back to an old tradition. Perhaps the brilliant idea came to an Italian housewife when she had cooked too much spaghetti. Imaginatively, she created a new speciality with the leftovers.

Serves 4
350 g/12 oz dried spaghetti
200 g/7 oz peeled, cooked prawns,
*   fresh or frozen*
1 bunch parsley
3 eggs
75 g/3 oz freshly grated
*   Parmesan cheese*
90 ml/6 tablespoons olive oil
salt and freshly ground white pepper

Approximately per portion:
2,700 kJ/640 kcal
38 g protein, 29 g fat
60 g carbohydrate

● Approximate preparation
   time: 30–45 minutes

1. Cook the spaghetti in salted boiling water until it is tender, but still firm to the bite. Strain, rinse with cold water and drain well.

2. Meanwhile, coarsely chop the prawns or leave them whole (thaw frozen prawns first). Finely chop the parsley.

3. Beat together the eggs, parsley and cheese in a large bowl until smooth. Stir in the prawns and season to taste with salt and pepper. Add the spaghetti and carefully mix it in.

4. Heat half the olive oil in a large frying pan. Tip in the pasta mixture and fry over a fairly low heat, shaking the pan from time to time, until it is light brown on the underside. Use a lid to help turn the omelette. Fry the other side in the remaining oil until golden and crispy. Serve immediately.

Tortellini alla panna

Tortellini in cream sauce

Quick

Serves 4
500 g/1 1/4 lb dried tortellini with
    meat filling or 800 g/1 3/4 lb fresh
    tortellini with meat filling
40 g/1 1/2 oz butter
250 ml/8 fl oz double cream
freshly grated nutmeg
about 75 g/3 oz freshly grated
    Parmesan cheese
salt

Approximately per portion:
3,300 kJ/790 kcal
25 g protein, 37 g fat
86 g carbohydrate

● Approximate preparation
   time:30 minutes

---

1. Cook the tortellini in salted boiling water until they are tender, but still firm to the bite. Remove from the pan with a ladle, set aside and keep warm.

2. Meanwhile, melt the butter with about 105 ml/7 tablespoons of the cream in a large flameproof casserole. Stir in the nutmeg and season to taste with salt.

3. Tip the tortellini into the casserole and mix together by gently shaking the casserole. Gradually add the grated Parmesan cheese and the remaining cream a spoonful at a time. Keeping moving the casserole so that the sauce becomes smooth and covers the tortellini evenly. Serve immediately straight from the casserole.

Variation

Tortellini con panna e noci
Finely chop 25–30 shelled walnuts. Gradually pour 250 ml/8 fl oz lightly warmed double cream on to them. Stir in 115 g/4 oz very soft, but not melted, butter until the mixture is smooth and creamy. Season with salt and pepper. Mix with the cooked drained tortellini and serve immediately.

Ravioli al pomodoro

Ravioli in tomato sauce

For guests

Serves 4
1 onion
1/2 bunch basil
2 x 400 g/14 oz cans tomatoes
120 ml/4 fl oz olive oil
pinch of ground peperoncino or
    cayenne pepper
pinch of sugar
1 bay leaf
500 g/1 1/4 lb dried ravioli with
    meat or cheese filling or 800 g/
    1 3/4 lb fresh ravioli with meat or
    cheese filling
salt
75 g/3 oz freshly grated
    Parmesan cheese

Approximately per portion:
2,300 kJ/550 kcal
26 g protein, 9 g fat
92 g carbohydrate

● Approximate preparation
   time: 1 hour

---

1. Finely dice the onion. Coarsely chop the basil. Put the tomatoes, together with their can juice, into a bowl and mash with a fork.

2. Heat 75 ml/5 tablespoons of the olive oil. Add the onion and sauté over a medium heat for 5 minutes. Add the tomatoes, peperoncino, sugar, bay leaf and basil and season to taste with salt. Cook, uncovered, until the sauce has thickened.

3. Cook the ravioli in salted boiling water with 15 ml/1 tablespoon of the remaining oil until it is tender, but still firm to the bite.

4. Remove the bay leaf from the sauce and discard. Stir in the remaining oil and adjust the seasoning if necessary.

5. Carefully mix the ravioli with the sauce in a warm serving dish or serve them separately. Hand the grated cheese separately.

Above: Tortellini alla panna
Below: Ravioli al pomodoro

Gnocchi alla trentina

Trentino-style dumplings

Serves 4
120 ml/4 fl oz milk
2 eggs
freshly grated nutmeg
115 g/4 oz freshly grated
 Parmesan cheese
25 g/1 oz plain flour
75 g/3 oz butter
salt and freshly ground black pepper

Approximately per portion:
2,500 kJ/ 600 kcal
25 g protein, 31 g fat
52 g carbohydrate

● Approximate preparation
 time: 1 hour

1. Heat the milk until it is lukewarm. Lightly beat the eggs. In a bowl, mix together 2.5 ml/ 1/2 teaspoon salt, a pinch of nutmeg, half the Parmesan cheese and the flour. Add the milk and the eggs and mix together to form a smooth dough.

2. Form small rolls from the dough about the thickness of a finger. Cut each roll into pieces about 3 cm/ 1 1/4 inch long.

3. Cook the gnocchi, a few at a time, in salted boiling water. When the gnocchi float to the surface, they are cooked. Remove with a slotted spoon, transfer to a warm serving dish and keep warm.

4. Melt the butter and immediately remove from the heat. Pour it over the gnocchi and sprinkle with the remaining grated Parmesan cheese. Season with pepper, mix well and serve immediately.

Gnocchi verdi

Spinach dumplings

Exquisite • Vegetarian

Serves 4
200 g/7 oz ricotta cheese
750 g/1 lb 10 oz spinach
115 g/4 oz butter
2 eggs
115 g/4 oz plain flour
115 g/4 oz freshly grated
 Parmesan cheese
freshly grated nutmeg
salt and freshly ground black pepper

Approximately per portion:
2,300 kJ/550 kcal
30 g protein, 36 g fat
24 g carbohydrate

● Approximate preparation
 time: 2 hours

1. Wrap the ricotta in muslin and squeeze out the whey, then mash it with a fork.

2. Put the spinach in a saucepan in just the water clinging to the leaves after washing. Cover and cook until it wilts. Drain and squeeze out as much water as possible. Chop the leaves finely.

3. Heat 25 g/1 oz of the butter in a flameproof casserole. Add the spinach and cook until dry. Stir in the ricotta and remove the casserole from the heat.

4. Lightly beat the eggs. Mix together the eggs, flour and about 25 g/1 oz of the grated Parmesan cheese to make a smooth paste. Stir in the spinach and season to taste with salt, pepper and nutmeg. Set aside in a cool place for about 45 minutes.

5. With floured hands, shape a walnut-size test dumpling. Melt half the remaining butter in an ovenproof dish. Cook the test dumpling in salted boiling water for 5–7 minutes. If the dumpling overcooks, knead some more flour into the dough.

6. Shape the remaining dumplings and cook them, a few at a time, in salted boiling water. Remove, drain and keep warm while you cook the remainder.

7. Preheat the oven to 240°C/475°F/Gas 9. Arrange the gnocchi in the prepared dish, sprinkle with the remaining grated Parmesan cheese and dot with the remaining butter. Bake in the oven until the cheese has melted. Serve immediately.

Above: Gnocchi alla trentina
Below: Gnocchi verdi

Great Little Cook Books
Pasta

Published originally under the title
Spaghetti by Gräfe und Unzer
Verlag GmbH, München

© 1990 by Gräfe und Unzer Verlag
GmbH, München

English-language edition
© 1998 by Transedition Limited,
Oxford, England

This edition published by
Aura Books plc

Translation:
Translate-A-Book, Oxford

Editing:
Linda Doeser

Typesetting:
Organ Graphic, Abingdon

10 9 8 7 6 5 4 3 2 1
Printed in Dubai

ISBN 1 901683 27 3

You will find the recipe for the dish on the front cover, pasta alla bolognese – pasta with meat sauce – on page 44.

Note:
For all recipes, ingredients are given in metric and imperial measurements. Follow only one set, as they are not interchangeable.

Odette Teubner
was taught by her father, the internationally renowned food photographer, Christian Teubner. After that she worked for some months as a fashion photographer. At present she works exclusively in the Teubner Studio for Food Photography. In her spare time she is an enthusiastic painter of children's portraits. She uses her own son as a model.

Kerstin Mosny
studied photography at a college in French-speaking Switzerland. After that she worked as an assistant to various photographers, including the food photographer, Jürgen Tapprich in Zürich. She now works in the Teubner Studio for Food Photography.

Marieluise Christl-Licosa
was born and grew up in the Tyrol. She lived for many years in Milan with her husband and four sons. There she learned to speak Italian and studied Italian cooking in its own country. Countless journeys and long holidays in all the different regions of Italy led to many friendly contacts with the Italian people.
   With real passion Mrs Christl-Licosa has collected recipes from Neapolitan fishermen, the wives of Piedmontese mountain farmers, leading cooks from Lombardy and Tuscany and, not least, from well-known chefs in the great cities. Since then, working in the kitchen has become her hobby. She teaches Italian at a college near Munich and holds weekend seminars on Italian cooking throughout Bavaria.